T0387414

INVASIVE SPECIES

ENGLISH IVY

by Alicia Z. Klepeis

pogo

Ideas for Parents and Teachers

Pogo Books let children practice reading informational text while introducing them to nonfiction features such as headings, labels, sidebars, maps, and diagrams, as well as a table of contents, glossary, and index.

Carefully leveled text with a strong photo match offers early fluent readers the support they need to succeed.

Before Reading

- "Walk" through the book and point out the various nonfiction features. Ask the student what purpose each feature serves.
- Look at the glossary together. Read and discuss the words.

Read the Book

- Have the child read the book independently.
- Invite him or her to list questions that arise from reading.

After Reading

- Discuss the child's questions. Talk about how he or she might find answers to those questions.
- Prompt the child to think more. Ask: English ivy spreads fast. It can keep native plants from growing. Can you think of any other plants that do this?

Pogo Books are published by Jump!
5357 Penn Avenue South
Minneapolis, MN 55419
www.jumplibrary.com

Copyright © 2023 Jump!
International copyright reserved in all countries.
No part of this book may be reproduced in any form without written permission from the publisher.

Library of Congress Cataloging-in-Publication Data

Names: Klepeis, Alicia, 1971- author.
Title: English ivy / by Alicia Z. Klepeis.
Description: Minneapolis, MN: Jump!, Inc., [2023]
Series: Invasive species | Includes index.
Audience: Ages 7-10
Identifiers: LCCN 2022014680 (print)
LCCN 2022014681 (ebook)
ISBN 9798885241014 (hardcover)
ISBN 9798885241021 (paperback)
ISBN 9798885241038 (ebook)
Subjects: LCSH: English ivy–Juvenile literature.
Invasive plants–Juvenile literature.
Classification: LCC SB615.E54 K54 2023 (print)
LCC SB615.E54 (ebook)
DDC 583/.44–dc23/eng/20220411
LC record available at https://lccn.loc.gov/2022014680
LC ebook record available at https://lccn.loc.gov/2022014681

Editor: Eliza Leahy
Designer: Emma Bersie
Content Consultant: Claudia S. Ingham, PhD, Animal and Rangeland Sciences, Oregon State University

Photo Credits: asharkyu/Shutterstock, cover; crystaldream/Shutterstock, 1; Scisetti Alfio/Shutterstock, 3; Shutterstock, 4; MacBen/Shutterstock, 5tl; Alena Charykova/Shutterstock, 5tr; Vlad Sokolovsky/Shutterstock, 5bl; Sara Mountain/Shutterstock, 5br; knelson20/Shutterstock, 6-7 (top); Zuzha/Shutterstock, 6-7 (bottom); Marina Denisenko/iStock, 8; Lagui/iStock, 9; Kq333/Shutterstock, 10-11; Andrii Lysenko/iStock, 12-13 (top); Gordon Miller/Dreamstime, 12-13 (bottom); Karel Bock/Shutterstock, 14-15tl; Pi-Lens/Shutterstock, 14-15tr; Nikolai Kurzenko/Dreamstime, 14-15bl; Elenic/Dreamstime, 14-15br; agefotostock/Alamy, 16-17 (top); Dietrich Leppert/Shutterstock, 16-17 (bottom); MYDAYcontent/Shutterstock, 18; SolStock/iStock, 19; Linda Davidson/The Washington Post/Getty, 20-21; GiorgioMagini/iStock, 23.

Printed in the United States of America at Corporate Graphics in North Mankato, Minnesota.

TABLE OF CONTENTS

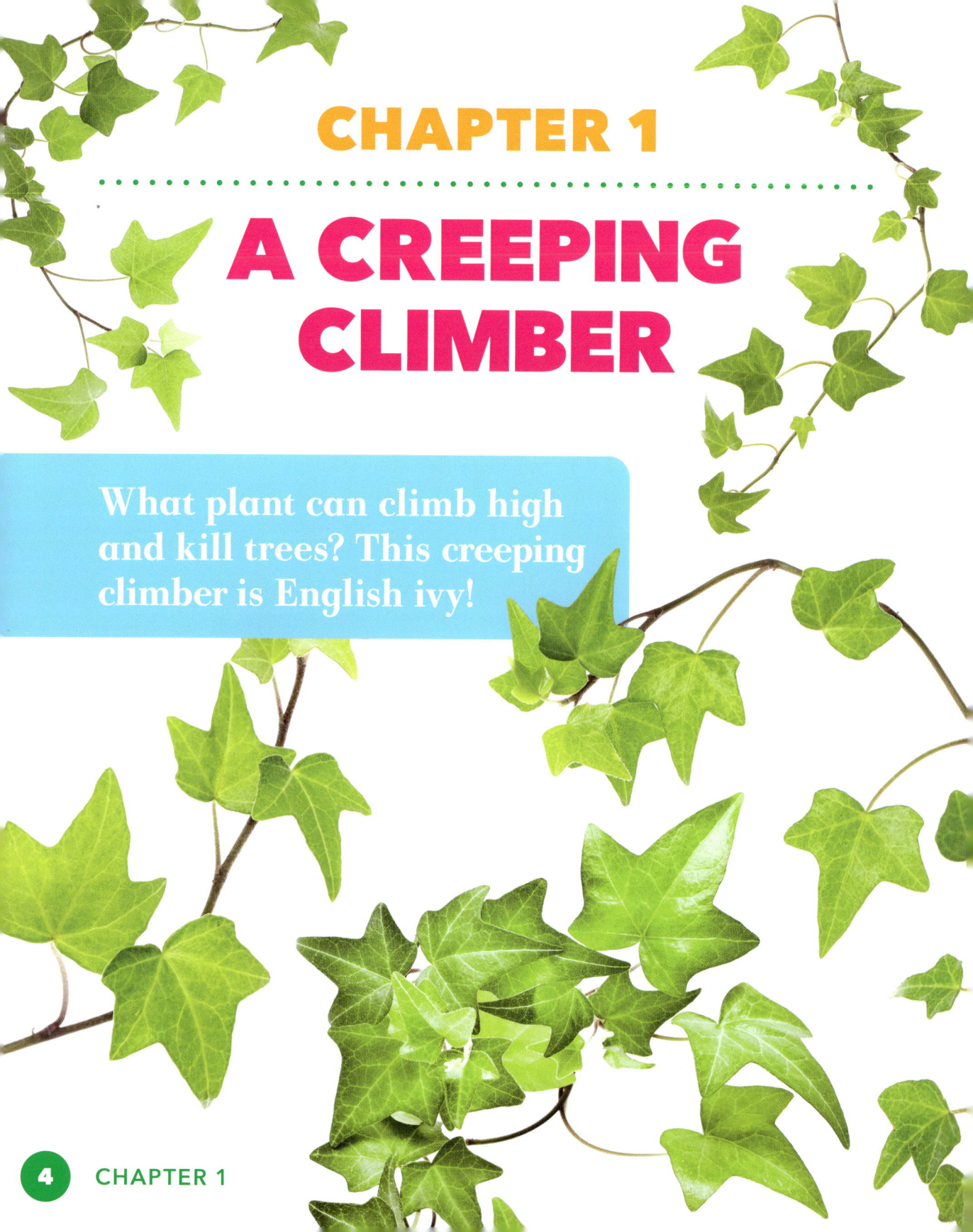

CHAPTER 1

A CREEPING CLIMBER

What plant can climb high and kill trees? This creeping climber is English ivy!

There are hundreds of kinds of English ivy. Many are green. Others are gray, yellow, or cream. Some are even pink or purple! The leaves can have streaks. Some have a marble pattern.

English ivy plants can be 50 feet (15 meters) across. The waxy leaves trail across the ground. They form a thick mat.

They also climb as they grow. They can grow 100 feet (30 m) tall! Some attach to trees. Others climb buildings.

DID YOU KNOW?

Adult English ivy plants produce flowers and fruit. The flowers are small. The fruit grows in clumps. It can look like a bunch of grapes.

CHAPTER 2

SUNLIGHT STEALERS

English ivy is **native** to Europe, western Asia, and northern Africa. It grows in forests and fields.

This plant **adapts** well. It can grow on hills. It grows in shady or sunny places. It can also grow in many kinds of soil. It can even survive **drought**!

Because English ivy adapts well, it spreads easily. It is an **invasive species** in North America. Here, it grows in many **habitats**, including forests and grasslands.

Colonists brought it here in the early 1700s. Why? They used it to decorate. They liked how it kept the ground green.

TAKE A LOOK!

In North America, English ivy is found in many U.S. states and parts of Canada. Take a look!

1 ALASKA

PACIFIC OCEAN

2 HAWAII

CANADA

UNITED STATES

GULF OF MEXICO

■ = English ivy invasive range

N
W — E
S

People still enjoy this plant. It is sold at **nurseries**. People plant it in their yards and gardens.

Animals eat the plant's fruit. They spread its seeds in their waste. The plant grows in new areas.

DID YOU KNOW?

Some states **ban** nurseries from selling English ivy. Oregon and Washington are two.

nursery

trillium

creeping dogwood

clematis

honeysuckle

When English ivy covers the ground, it stops other plants from getting sunlight and water. Native plants like trillium and creeping dogwood can't grow.

English ivy also causes problems when it climbs. It can **smother** native climbing plants like clematis and honeysuckle.

English ivy also climbs tree trunks. It surrounds a tree's branches. It blocks sunlight from the tree's leaves. Lower branches die first. Then, higher branches die. The tree becomes weaker. Eventually, it dies.

This ivy can damage buildings it grows on, too. How? Its roots can widen cracks in stone or wood. This lets in **moisture**.

CHAPTER 3

GETTING RID OF IVY

Scientists study English ivy. They study the plants it harms. They look at what animals eat it. They **track** where it spreads. This helps us understand where it could spread next.

Many people work to stop the spread of English ivy. They pull the plants from the ground. They cut vines that climb trees.

Goats can be trained to eat English ivy. This can help get rid of the plants. And the goats get a filling meal!

English ivy hurts native plants and animals. We must try to stop it from spreading. How can you help? Spread the word about English ivy. Dig up ivy plants near you. Native plants and animals will thank you!

DID YOU KNOW?

English ivy can cause a rash. Always wear gloves when touching it. The fruit is dangerous to people and pets if eaten.

ACTIVITIES & TOOLS

PLANTS NEAR YOU

Many native plants in North America are in danger because of English ivy. Learn more about native plants in your area in this fun activity!

What You Need:

- books and magazines or a computer
- sheets of paper
- colored markers, pencils, or crayons
- glue or tape
- posterboard or large sheet of paper

1. Use print sources or a computer to learn about what plants are native where you live. Choose two.

2. Find out what these two plants look like and how big they grow.

3. Draw one of the plants on a piece of paper. Record how large it gets. Repeat this step for the other plant you chose.

4. Glue or tape your drawings to your posterboard.

5. What are some similarities between the native plants you researched and English ivy? What are some differences?

GLOSSARY

adapts: Changes to fit a new situation.

ban: To officially forbid something or prevent someone from doing something.

colonists: People who live in or help to establish a new territory.

drought: A long period without rain.

habitats: The places where animals or plants are usually found.

invasive species: Any kind of living organism that is not native to a specific area.

moisture: Wetness, as from rain, snow, dew, or fog.

native: Growing or living naturally in a particular area of the world.

nurseries: Places that sell trees, plants, and seeds.

smother: To cover something thickly or entirely.

track: To follow and try to find a plant by looking for marks or traces of it.

INDEX

adapts 9, 10

animals 12, 18, 21

ban 12

branches 16

buildings 6, 16

climb 4, 6, 15, 16, 19

colonists 10

drought 9

fields 8

flowers 6

forests 8, 10

fruit 6, 12, 21

goats 21

grasslands 10

moisture 16

native 8, 15, 21

nurseries 12

range 11

rash 21

scientists 18

soil 9

spreads 10, 12, 18, 19, 21

track 18

trees 4, 6, 16, 19

TO LEARN MORE

Finding more information is as easy as 1, 2, 3.

1. Go to www.factsurfer.com
2. Enter "Englishivy" into the search box.
3. Choose your book to see a list of websites.

FACT SURFER